salmonpoetry

Publishing Irish & International
Poetry Since 1981

After The Fall
BRIAN KIRK

Published in 2017 by
Salmon Poetry
Cliffs of Moher, County Clare, Ireland
Website: www.salmonpoetry.com
Email: info@salmonpoetry.com

ISBN 978-1-910669-99-0

COVER PHOTOGRAPHY: Jessie Lendennie
AUTHOR PHOTOGRAPH: Martha Kirk
COVER DESIGN & TYPESETTING: *Siobhán Hutson*

Printed in Ireland by Sprint Print

*Salmon Poetry gratefully acknowledges the support of
The Arts Council / An Chomhairle Ealaoín*

For Laura

Acknowledgements

Acknowledgement is due to the editors of the following publications in which a number of these poems, or versions of them, have appeared:
Abridged; Southword; The Irish Times; The Raintown Review; Skylight 47; Crannóg Magazine; The Ofi Press; Shot Glass Journal; The Stony Thursday Book; Bare Hands Poetry; Boyne Berries; Burning Bush 2; Café Review; Can Can; Live Encounters; Ropes Anthology; Revival; Honest Ulsterman; The First Cut; The Blue Max Review; Night and Day Anthology; Three Drops Press Anthology; The Lion Tamer Dreams of Office Work.

"The Man, The Boy And The Map" won the 2014 Jonathan Swift Poetry Competition; "New Year" won the 2015 Bailieborough Poetry Competition; "Birthday" won the 2016 Galway Rape Crisis Centre Poetry Competiton; "God Of Love" was placed second in the formal category of the 2017 Poetry On The Lake Poetry Competition; "The Couple" was highly commended in the Robert Monteith Poetry Competition 2017; "Somewhere In Between" was placed third in the 2016 North West Words Poetry Competition; "Orienteering" was nominated for the Forward Prize 2015; "Life is Elsewhere" was commended in the Galway University Hospital Arts Trust Poetry Competition in 2014; "To Youth" was nominated for a Pushcart Prize 2015; "Earthbound" was shortlisted in the Fermoy International Poetry Competition 2013; "Taking Simple Vows" was highly commended in the iYeats Poetry Competition 2012; "Broken Love" was highly commended in the Bare Hands International Poetry Competition 2012; "Still" was highly commended in the iYeats Poetry Competition 2011; "Shallow Grave" was commended in the Padraic Fallon Poetry Competition 2008.

My thanks to the Arts Office of South Dublin County Council for a bursary received while writing the collection.

I wish to extend my thanks to John Murphy who has been a reader and mentor throughout the compilation of this collection. Thanks also go to my fellow poets at the Hibernian Poetry Workshop whose advice and encouragement are always appreciated. Particular thanks go to Colm Keegan, Breda Wall Ryan, Amanda Bell, Annemarie Ní Churreáin, Michael O'Loughlin, Alan Jude Moore and Tony Higgins. I wish to thank Jessie Lendennie and Siobhán Hutson at Salmon Poetry for making the dream a reality.

I'd like to thank my family for their continuing patience and unflagging support.

Contents

After The Fall

Somewhere east of Eden
gorged in a blind moment,
lips lost between wet lips,
tongues tasting summer fruit
before it ripened.
Afterwards – transfigured
in the other's eyes –
we recognised our teenage selves
as something more than
hungry looks, black-nailed
fingers seeking yielding flesh.
The residue of that first kiss
upon our lips
like a bruise
we can test,
reminding us of
our twin staples:
lack and appetite.

Two Foxes

Outside the thunder died to rain
and still the air sat heavy
against the lifted sash,
miming a glassless pane.
Back and front thrown open,
connecting door shoe-wedged,
not a breath between two rooms
to stir a leaf of paper or a map
open on the table.

Islington.

Our children slept in silence
in an unmade bed
while we sipped wine and read.
The traffic on the wet streets
came and went, insistent,
anonymous
as only cities are.

Did we remember – separately, silently –
nights in other flats
on different streets,
before or after thunder storms,
before our world was formed,
our hopes agreed, when promises
we made out loud
tamed the seas and
caused the winds to drop?
For years we drifted on the tide
of love or obligation
and washed up where we started out:
in a city foreign and familiar,
tentative, trusting,
unafraid.

One floor up the glow
of a red traffic light
was the sun rising.
The roar of engines and shouts
from the street was drowned in the downpour
after midnight —
perhaps soon the city would sleep.
A voice, loud and strangled,
ripped from the lungs,
closed my book.
I looked down on the wet street.
And then you were beside me,
wonder and fear in your eyes
because you heard it too.
Then we saw them: *Oh look!*
Two foxes running down
Barnsbury Road.

Their coats were coal-grey
under streetlight,
their tails lank and ragged,
their heads sharp and pensive.
The dog looked at his mate
and we looked at each other.
Then we heard it close by —
engine revving.
He shot off in panic
under our window, while she
darted into the park.
A single car passed.
The sharp squeal of brakes.
Nothing stirred, we didn't speak,
but we looked up and down the dark street
till we saw her quick head
poke through the park railings.
She sniffed the night air
and cried out,
but he did not come.

We stood at the window
long after she'd gone.
It was late, and the morning
was already making demands.
We undressed saying little,
but telling ourselves
she was not crying really,
just calling as animals do.
We stood over the children in silence
before we put out the light.
You kissed me
while cars came and went
through the rain
and I knew I would never forget
the night we saw foxes on Barnsbury Road,
and remembered our love in the body,
the skin and the blood
on a wet London street.

Tryst

At the edge of night
by the side wall of a pub
masked by the blank stare
of a broken street lamp,
hands buried in pockets
he waits,
kicking small stones
from under his feet.

Unseen, he watches a door
swallow men one by one.
A slurred racket escapes
now and then,
clouting his cold ears
like the dull clang of
an ominous bell
intoning his future.

Past shuttered shops and
boys who make catcalls
she walks to the spot
where they meet,
feeling the cold of the town
in her stomach,
but not on her legs
which are bare.

He steps out of the gloom,
dark as the devil.
His cold hands on her face
as they kiss
bring a queer warmth
that is not from within,
as the night sucks them in
one on one to the wall.

Persephone

She walked into the Sheaf of Wheat
one night and disappeared.

The barman found her grainy image
on CCTV for the police,

but she was gone without a trace.
Two weeks later the place burned down,

guard dogs silenced with a cut of meat
spiked by a shadowed figure in a cap.

Some say there was a smell of sulphur,
others got a whiff of shite.

Bones

If you could see yourself
at nineteen
not in a studied attitude
but in repose
you might appreciate
the potency of
superficiality
not be so quick
to disavow
the lascivious eye
the lustrous hair
the easy pull of sinew
on strong bone
the sheen of skin
that hides so well
a sleeping skeleton

Life Is Elsewhere

Even the sound of a goods train
passing in the night,
rattling the rotten frame
of my childhood window;
even that spoke to me then
of a life I was missing.
Later, the dead eyes of a stranger
on the bus home from school,
unshaven and shabby in creased overcoat,
a worn paperback in his pocket;
he lived the life I both feared and desired.
Or the men who stood on the
doorsteps of pubs, or bookmakers,
cigarettes hidden in hands with stained fingers;
these were the ones I yearned to be counted among –
not the good, the polite and the young.
But I was bound by the kindness of others,
obliged to be who I was
out of duty and love;
I had to create out of nothing
false reasons to fight
where no fight was sought,
to reject all that was given for free
in a house where I knew only love.

Habanera

Summer is over,
but the glassy glow of late-afternoon sun
speaks of the south
as I lie on the bed
watching you dress.
I am tired but my eyes are wide open,
woken to a moment thought lost:
a basement room in Tyndale Terrace,
a sallow girl dressing
for a Cuban night on the tiles.
Downstairs the children's voices
call a name I hardly recognise.
You stand in a daze by the mirror
and twenty years have passed
without our knowing.
I rise to go to them,
press past your naked body
in the narrow room.
I stop and fold my arms around you
and feel a boyish yearning
to resume the habanera
started all those years ago,
but you recoil –
you have to be somewhere.
Already I hear steps upon the stairs.

Chameleon

I have lived in big cities,
ridden buses and trains,
and travelled by airplane
all over the place.
I think myself modern,
smart, cynical even.
I am mouthy, opinionated,
sometimes without justification.
Don't know why, I just am.

>   I don't like it:
>   the noise of the traffic,
>   the unceasing race to maintain
>   the lie of our self-importance.

I have lived in the country,
picked spuds and tomatoes,
topped turnips, cut cabbage
on cold winter mornings
swimming in oilskins.
I have savoured cigarettes
on headlands among men
with damn all to say.
Ages ago, but still me.

>   I don't like it:
>   the slowness of Nature,
>   the dullness of life strapped to
>   her wheel as she grinds.

Now I move between city
and country with ease,
pretending in each to be
of the other. In fact I am
neither, heritage
long ago given away;

careless of the past
I thought my future could be
plucked from the air. I was wrong.

> I don't like it:
> the way I so easily
> talk when I know I should keep
> my mouth shut.

Gulliver In The Glass House

Lying on your back among the rows of plants,
eyes closed, listening to the Yahoos jabber on.
Soon they'll be throwing stones. The pump cranks up,
feeds water through tubes to plants ranged
in their grow bags, leaves lifted to the sky.
Open your eyes to the concave glare and you are
driving down a canopied road in search of ancient images,
the sky obscured by vernal light. The past comes
rushing with the sound of passing trains and city roars;
a gaping door is banging in the wind, it opens
onto farm yards from your youth, and their attendant
dead machinery. You emerge from darkness to a subdued light,
a murky cavern reaching into the realm of memory.
The image tells a tale but not the truth, the truth will come
in time out of a candle-lit anteroom and down into
a darkened cave eternally. It started with a
nagging pain, a doctor's scrawl upon a page;
you lie still on your back under a radiant crown,
you try to block the sounds until the images converge
and you are back again beneath tomato vines.

Birthday

(for Laura)

You ask if there's a gift I'd like to mark the passing year,
but how can I demand – no more than you can give –
the turning back of time to when I knew you first?

Not back to the doorway of the Red Cow Inn, when drunk
I pecked you on the cheek and mumbled happy birthday;
not, one year later, when we sat with friends in the Green Man

on St. Martin's Lane and I stayed quiet, sober. Not back
to when you met me from the train at Euston after my father died,
or sometime after that, when we moved to Highbury on our own;

when we began to drop our masks and make our true selves known.
I think of how we wallowed in our love for years
before the kids arrived and stole our time but gave us

so much more. I was always stealing things,
books from shops, kisses in the backs of taxis,
always wanting something more when I had plenty.

I feared love then, considered it a failing, a retreat, until
I felt it. Though it was buried deep you disinterred
it, breathed life into its musty lungs and made it sing.

I see you as Prometheus, a kind of Doctor Frankenstein
to my ignoble monster, but you did not abandon me when
I reverted to base nature, when others bayed for blood.

You took me back to Dublin and the children came;
they taught me over time to do new things,
to stay up nights and cool a fever, heat a bottle

or simply sit and let the long hours shorten into day.
I want the long hours back but you can't give me that.
Sometimes I yearn to go back even further,

to a world defined by family, fields and railway tracks,
the sham abandon of the long school holidays.
I want the days to be mid-summer all year long,

those childhood games that lasted until darkness fell
and twilight was a midnight walk back home with
a ball at my feet and my head completely empty.

Each night I close my eyes and we are young again, before time
dragged us down its hungry maw. On waking I can feel I'm falling,
but reaching out into the dark I find you, hold on tight.

Sleep

Close the door, but leave the window open
so we can hear the distant shouts
of children, barking dogs, car engines dropping
gear to make a turn. We'll lie a little longer
while the house is ours alone.
Listen to the tapping of the blind against
the sash and close your eyes,
but leave your heart wide open so I can
whisper things I typically forget to say
like thank you, love you, miss you
even when you're only hours away. Don't
be concerned, let engines, dogs and voices
chorus rapture while we sleep.

New Year

Unlock the doors and let the east wind sing
between the table legs and upturned chairs.
Let dust unsettle on a belt of air
that binds the living to the rising spring
and stirs the sheets that cover everything.
The books you haven't read are all still there,
the clothes you left behind unworn are where
you left them – let them be, you'll never bring
the past to life again. Ignore the sting
of memory or the urge to say a prayer;
what you are doing should not prompt despair.
Take a deep breath, roll up your sleeves and swing
the hammer at the past and have no fear;
level the ground, make straight, this is New Year.

Evening Commute

Sun sweats gold between September trees
and buildings cower under ancient clouds;
buses clog impatient streets, half-hearted
carriers of tired evening crowds.

Street-lights come on before there is a need
as if winter can't come soon enough;
it makes you pull your coat around yourself
and shiver in your seat beside the gruff

companion on your journey home who taps
his phone, neglecting humankind,
another wage slave making his way home
who stares into his hand but who is blind

to life; how the dark will bleed into the day,
the stops where noisy school kids will alight.
You wonder does he know time's steady march
will pause neither for him nor traffic light.

What world awaits him when he shuts the door?
Do children's faces brighten when he speaks?
Or do they run and hide at his approach,
do harsh words send tears rolling down soft cheeks?

You notice harried faces in the street,
stray dogs sniff bins, move on, return and piss.
The traffic thickens now, you're marking time
between the stops and starts, the air brake's hiss.

He rises to get off, pockets his phone,
and you are woken from your idle dreams
of other lives that you will never know.
Rain falls, it runs across the glass in streams.

Passion Spent

Years pass
you never notice
how the world changes
obsessed by yourself
time seeps
sweating the hours
as if waiting
for something to start
though you know
the first act is over
the second
almost done

Your love
was the climax
or nadir
it's hard to tell
one from the other
no fucking
no fighting
you long for drama
but there is none
beyond the sun setting
the moon
coming up

The night
was your time
to shine
out of shadow
you conjured desire
and jealousy
in equal parts
until the beating
of your heart
occluded everything
and your breath
came short

Broken Love

When she was gone
he felt her presence keenly;
her cold hands chafed
his naked flesh at night
until her mark was on his body,
her taste in his dry mouth.
He spoke to her and
in the silence heard
her whispered words:
I forgive you, you forgive me.

When she returned
he missed her in every room;
side by side on the sofa
she was too close to touch.
He longed for her body,
lust sharpened by lack
but stifled by fear.
He turned up the TV.
If I stop loving you
will you stop loving me?

Earthbound

The day declines
in the way
it always does
with drink and cigarette
in hand

You long to kiss
those lips
but won't
and when you speak
you always say
the things you know
you shouldn't

It is a knack
of yours
to complicate
the natural beauty
of a sunset
to mar the brilliance
of a star-filled night
with reckless words

You never look
beyond the rooftops
never see the sky
you love the dirt
and you belong
earthbound
always looking down

Leave-taking

(for Eddie)

The five years before he died
you took him back each spring
to where he started out;
small towns on the Louth-Monaghan
border that burned on the tongue
with bucolic satisfaction –
Knockbridge, Inniskeen, Rosslough –
places I only knew in imagination.
Each year you drove him down
the high-hedged roads, slowing
only to look into derelict yards
or fields where people he once knew
had worked and lived.

One year, before you turned for home,
you stopped in Art McCooey's bar
where, in the grip of whiskey,
there were words and you were privy to
another side of Pa, a man not known for talk.
You had to drag him out after a while
and put him in the car; he had grown
fierce, rubbed up against a face
from the dim past, an incident
arising at a dance in the dawn of time;
the hurt still raw, the anger in his eyes.
You knew you couldn't ask,
so drove the whole way home in silence.

Then that last year, it was as if he knew;
he made you stop at every neighbour's house,
although you'd passed them all before
for four years in a row. You let him go,
waited in the car and read a book
while he was feted by farmers and their wives
like one who'd been away at war for years,
wondering what his business could be now
beyond the final saying of goodbyes.
When he emerged you saw a kind of light
in him, but didn't mention it.
On the way back, in McCooey's, whiskey in hand,
you held a sputtering match to his cigar.

Somewhere In Between

My brothers were out in the fields,
my sisters in the kitchen with our aunt
while I was somewhere in between,
hunting for eggs buried in warm hay

in and around the outlying sheds.
I wasn't strong enough to lift bales,
couldn't be trusted with a pitchfork;
even my soft hands were lethal,

dropping near-hatched eggs on flags.
I carried awkward buckets
from the pump across the yard,
socks squelching in wellies

when I reached the kitchen door.
I envied the older boys who rode
the old Dexta up and down drills
with steady hands.

One day they let me have a go.
I crushed plants in their prime,
red-faced, couldn't steer, couldn't hear
my uncle's roars of *knock her off!* –

mind-wandered to a distant bird
that could have been a cuckoo.
From then on I was useless,
fit company only for poor blind Pete

who sat at the back door stirring
only when rain began to fall, growling
when stray hens encroached.
At dinner-time in the noisy heat,

amid the sweat of hunger-driven men,
the food grew in my mouth as I chewed,
and when I took a drink to force it down
I gagged, the creamy yellow warmth

too much like nature, too unlike me.
I wanted only to be older then,
but by the time I got there
everything had changed.

Senseless

(i.m. Gerry Flanagan)

There is nothing more to say but still we talk,
as if the silence is a trapdoor into another world,
letting the dead come back to haunt us. He lives on,

but only as an idea in our minds and we explain away
his death although we know it is beyond explaining.
The crude fact of how he died is like a light

that can't be quenched. Although we didn't find him,
the image of his hanging shadow darkens our thoughts.
We can no longer picture him as he was, but we must see him

joyless, lifeless as a doll with empty eyes gazing into a future
he'll never meet. Our experience of the stench of death is
limited to the contents of the compost bin at home, we dig it

into the soil in spring, renewing the face of the earth.
It's easy to believe the idea of new growth when you smell
the sap rising, but fresh cut grass from weekend lawns

soon decays; it doesn't live again, it's new grass every time.
A Halloween false face mounted on a horizontal suit; that's how
he looks to us. We can't touch him, afraid there will be nothing

under his jacket sleeve; his scarecrow self is out of reach.
I watch a girl lean across the coffin and let her red lips
brush his quickly. I want to tell her he's not there.

Who does she think she's kissing? What does she taste on him?
The chemicals they use to make him fit for viewing or the vestiges
of misspent youth; cigarettes and alcohol, and fish and chips?

Rotten Apples

born too late
    at end of day
the dead apples
    fall
blown by the wind
    laid out
on corrugated tin
    covered against
gunmetal rain
    gathering
a fine dust
    of winter flies
turning
    I can
        smell them still

Red

The colour of war and of warmth,
of Christmas and the blood of martyrs,
the poppy of remembrance and the wine
that Lethe-like augurs oblivion.
When I was a child Reds hid under beds,
but I slept soundly, knowing there were
russet apples in the bowl at Halloween
when leaves decayed to rust and books were
read in secret under covers in the night.
Red means stop, and to go completely mad –
red mist, a red rag to a bull.
It is sin or sex, or life or beauty,
the shepherd's delight or perhaps a warning,
depending on the sky being red at night
or in the morning.

Young People

Town is the worst. I see them sitting at tables outside
smart bars, drinking strong liquor, lighting French cigarettes
while they talk with intensity about something I know

to be frivolous. They are bright-faced and healthy, white
teeth flashing smiles as they dip their heads in communion,
receiving the shared wisdom of like-minded souls.

How do they live with such poise? Can they not see me
pass by, the forced march of long life blistering feet, the
worries of working and money etched on my brow?

They are like stars, blinding themselves with their own
light eternally, celestial bodies orbiting my world in ways
I could never describe. They are as strange as the sun

at midnight, beautiful, restless, empty photons; they dazzle
me in my perpetual night.

Trinity

When I am dead you will not think of me
save on those days when it is customary,
birthdays, anniversaries, solemn days
when you will be obliged to find new ways
to make my presence felt again – absent
though I'll be. Fleetingly you'll be content
to let me rise, a spectre from the past;
rueful that I will never see the last
rays of the sun at end of day when all
my family – living and dead – lay down to fall
asleep in Christ or bed. Oh there was love
to spare albeit stored at one remove.
When I am dead I will be loved the most,
I will be father, son and holy ghost.

Paraphernalia

The inconsequential things a woman was allowed to keep:
a dead corsage in an antique wooden box,
a flimsy clasp to judge her secrets' worth.

An artichoke in lurid oils, a jar of cream to keep the years at bay,
a ribbon that she wore when she was happy once –
it cannot hold the past.

The last few letters that he wrote before he stopped.
A lip-sticked cigarette end in a cup that once held tea,
a half read novel of the cheapest kind.

Some coins, a list of things she never did.
Grey photographs of old people when they were young.
A cracked mirror to reflect her neverness.

Funerals

In some parts of the world before the feasting starts,
before the drinks are poured, a libation for the dead
is spilled on arid ground. Some people value those
who came before, but we know better.
Old stories are nothing more than wives' tales
and when we perish we rot in the ground,
go back to nature in the meanest way.
At funerals the one least present is always
the deceased; we do not see the dead among us,
guiding us, reminding us of who we are
and where we're from. We eat and drink,
laugh and kiss, lives flavoured by our loss,
all aches and joys endured or relished
in the shadow of a closing door.

Resurrection

Once a year
we hold back time
to brighten the morning;
we succumb to night
in the afternoon
at a price.

The sun slides
from the sky,
plays dead in twilight,
and for a moment we are
mute savages again,
doubting reason.

We tend to flickering
gods and demons,
afraid of our own shadows
hunched and awful
stalking us. All winter
we sustain the body

with roasted meat
and sticky sweets,
the soul with stories
half-hoped or half-believed in;
promises of new life
when the sun comes up.

God Of Love

When Abraham dragged Isaac up the mount
did he not pause a while to count
the times he'd kissed the child and held him close?
Or did he soldier on and pity those
who did not have the big man's ear like him,
who never had the pleasure of God's whim
imposed on them? It's hard to understand
how any god would raise a father's hand
against his child. The self-styled God of love
was not content with metaphor, a dove
was not enough, there should be suffering;
seared flesh, a beating heart from which to wring
the last few drops of blood — with his consent —
until his son was beaten up and spent.

Repetition

There is nothing in this world as beautiful as repetition,
it promises another morning, another night, another kiss;
it knows the answer to every question you can ask,
each moment is a memory of the future.

There is nothing in this world as terrible as repetition,
it threatens torture already meted out, it opens
wounds, revealing scars you thought were healed,
it tells you not to hope and points to history.

There is nothing in this world as beautiful as repetition,
reassuring you of what you think you know; each day
your god pulls down the sun and turns his night light on
so you can sleep in safety.

There is nothing in this world as terrible as repetition;
the wheel of life is turned by ignorance, desire and hate
and you become another — human or hungry ghost —
dying to the symmetry of things, to beauty.

Shallow Grave

I never thought that I would find him
cold and dead, stretched out in a stranger's yard,
as if sleeping – but not sleeping – numb, hard
as the frozen ground, draped in a fine skim
of winter's leavings. Only an old cat,
an insignificant death you might say –
Aristotle certainly saw it that way –
when compared to a human life lost; that
is what vexes some people, that feline
or canine can be treated like human,
cried over like lovers, valued like someone
you lived with and loved throughout their decline.
The divine in me with apt insouciance
digs a shallow grave and buries nuisance.

Simple Vows
Stat crux dum volvitur orbis

After you left I never spoke again
except to pray your name to God at night.

In morning's frozen breath I savoured you
as I relearned the anguish of the habit.

Beyond the Hermitage I dreamed you close,
among new leaves your smile was apple bright.

All day I walked the Liturgy of the Hours
till Mass, when in the altered Host I relished you.

Immanent

There's a certain way
the twilight seems to linger
after darkness falls,
before the street lights
smudge the evening sky
and open up the night
to tired eyes.
The past arrives unnoticed,
nameless, aged,
dragging child-worries
in its wake, muted,
tear-stained, washed
in sudden gloom
beneath the trees
that seem to bend
and snatch unspoken words
from yawning mouths.
The night is ready
like a cat to pounce,
and idly, like a cat,
it paws the moment
that has passed
and toys with it
till it expires.

To Youth

The day will come when you will want to leave
your home and family and your friends behind.
You will not stop to wonder or to grieve,
new days will open out inviting blind
pursuit of dreams that probably won't come true,
or if they do, then not the way you planned.
Yes, I am old and cynical, but you
are young; a year is like a grain of sand
that falls unnoticed in your hourglass life.
Success is so apparent you can taste
the wine, hear the applause, ignore the knife
that warns of hurt to follow, interlaced
with tears and laughter, boredom and the rest
that makes our lives so blundering, so blessed.

The Couple

Terribly self-conscious most of the time,
she tried to be like all the other wives
who only held opinions that would chime
with husbands who lived honest, busy lives.
But she was brighter than the others knew,
a liberated woman who held sway.
He understood her love was something few
would ever know, and fewer could repay.
A gentleness belied her force of mind
which he was grateful for in times of stress
when he could give himself and be entwined
with her and find his better self. And yes,
they stole strength from each other as they went,
a lifetime's give and take, some discontent.

The Flowering Of Age

After insipid youth's
    impotent rage and rant
comes calm; empowering,
    just, engendered by
the flowering of age,
    the afterburn of energies
expended in pursuit of
    money, love, sex —
or all of the above —
    supplanted by the
certainty that there is
    only doubt to speak of:
conviction is by choice
    and likely moot.

Still

Still in my dreams
I search for him.
I lower a knotted rope,
secured by blood,
into the pit where I was raised,
climb down, inch by inch,
until I reach the bottom,
plunder the remains
of half-written histories,
the skeletons of childhood pets,
the shadowed photographs
of summers in warm clothes.

That day in the pub
in Canning Town, after he died,
still trying to play the hard chaw
among real villains.
We sat on in silence after they left.
All my bragging was done,
I was tired and hungover.
I wished I could cry, but I couldn't,
not then. Not till much later
when we were alone in my room,
on the bed, worn out,
with the lights off, no sound,
a single thread of come
connecting us to the world.
I waited for a ripple to stir
the surface of a pond,
a tiny sign of life as it is lived by others,
but I gave you only tears,
the inarticulate sobs of the habitually scared.

Ouija

Back then we had no doubt that things
went on behind the veil of humdrum days.
In school we sensed our teacher's other life,
his loving or rebelling kids, his father
disappointed, his mother drunk,
wife disappeared long years.

We knew there was eternal life
even though we never saw a Lazarus;
we knew someone who knew the man
who'd seen the spectre at the big house
take the brush from a workman's hand
when he tried to paint the blue room green.

But passing time brought only doubts,
and we were always seeking proof
like Thomas, fingers poised to press
the flesh of the risen dead, imagining
the satisfaction we would feel
confirming blunt substantiation.

We found a photo in a library book –
a board that was a portal to the spirits –
and so we had to make our own; taking
time to make the letters and numbers clear,
we carved a heart-shaped planchette
from a lettered wooden block

and we began. When we questioned our ghost
the pointer duly moved under our touch,
but we'd grown cynical by then, suspecting
one another of pretending divination in the
darkened room. But when a flaming coal spat
out onto the rug we fled like true believers.

Song

The morning
welcomes broken song
from restless birds.
While the others
are in bed
you whistle.

Song is wasted
on afternoons
when the hours
lie side by side
like islands
in a tranquil sea.

At evening
as sky closes in
your voice rises up
to meet it
shimmering
in dense air.

But at night
you dive down
deep to find
your voice at
the bottom of a well
that is silent.

At The Archive Reading Room

Step off the street into the silence,
climb the stairs, produce your card
and push into the past.
Directories and almanacs,
old books and manuscripts,
lie waiting in repose for invocation,
your mark upon a chit of paper.
Withered maps and photographs,
guidebooks from a distant time,
ephemera of one kind or another
are wheeled along on soundless trolleys,
quickened, photocopied, browsed, returned,
temperature controlled.

Here you will find
your faceless ancestors
buried in dusty books,
in boxes on marked shelves,
under the dead leaves
of never-read pamphlets
and dog-eared photographs.

Readers are advised to take care
when handling manuscripts,
pencils only can be used for taking notes.
Archive materials are fragile, often irreplaceable,
so you are requested not to write on them,
not to lean on them,
not to place any object on top of them.
Record-keeping is an art,
not an act of administration.
Keep conversation to a minimum,
turn off your mobile phone or silence it.

Sit quietly and wait until
the flat file of their disaster
opens out across your desk:
the sundered walls, the roof collapsed,
the salty tears of barefoot children
washing dirty faces.

Time is passing. Ineluctably the
wheels will turn, the walls will fall,
all things will keep, tears dry in time.

A Memory

I can see my father sitting
behind me to the right
on the old couch in the big kitchen
at the edge of my peripheral vision.
A torn envelope open on one lap,
the Irish Press racing page
on the other, a biro poised.
I can't see his face,
but the blue serge of his uniform
reassures.
Cap pushed back
on his oiled head,
he scribbles the day's bets
between the up and down trains.

At night I am snug in the dark
beneath his old railway overcoat.
Light breaks from the kitchen;
I feel the hot rub of his day-old beard
on my baby face
last thing before sleep.

The Death Of Idealism

The bright talk of past days
unspools to slurs;
it was only a matter of time
before we gave in or gave up.
You could say we were born for it,
the slow decay into silence
but it isn't quite silence,
or acquiescence – it's more
like suppression, a self-imposed
stifling of speech,
maiming the words
as they come
(and they come)
for the mind is still bright
before speech. In secret
it uselessly wins the old spat
with itself while the tongue
lolls in a mouth
misshapen by fear.

The Lovers In Wartime

We lock the door and turn the lights down low,
pull down the shade and veil the world outside,
as if that might protect us from the slow
but creeping certainty, the scarlet tide
that washes us in guilt no one can bear,
and so we keep our distance, half the globe.
The ones who shout the loudest say they care,
the silent ones – the lovers – will not probe
the words of leaders for the core of truth
we know does not exist. We have our love,
we have no choice – as summer chooses youth
so we embrace the blindness, rise above
the unreality of distant war –
we are in love, we do not ask what for.

Town Foxes

How did we get here, knowing what we are
        and what we need to live?
This place we call home
        offers us nothing but still we remain,
scavenging and cowering by turns
        among hostile hosts.

They call us vermin, rabid plague-ridden curs,
        and would have us slaughtered,
where once they named us noble,
        cunning, wily, even sly.
Now we are foreign to our natures, delirious,
        fearful to the last,
        unwanted immigrants.

Commission

I've been instructed to compose these lines,
designed to quench the light and to deflect
with polite meaningless words, not underline
regret about your plight, nor to resurrect
it. People like you always have a case
to make, against the state, the church – abuse
you claim (which we all know was commonplace).
And so I'm charged with making an excuse
for other's failings such as they may be,
an expression of sorrow, not of guilt,
careful to sidestep liability
while at the same time stitching a dark quilt
to smother the words of those without a voice,
using the same language as Yeats and Joyce.

Helpless

You are not to be trusted, concealing
yourselves in airless containers,
massing at borders, demanding shelter
and food as if these were your rights;
infesting the lands of our neighbours,
over-running the peaceful inhabitants.
Our satellites descry your hydra heads
among the Adriatic waves, off Greece
in the Ionian Sea, while we remain
helpless against your onslaught.
Closer and closer you come, white-eyed,
brown arms extended in a show of force,
but – stranger than strange –
the nearer you approach
the smaller you become to us.

Stateless

It's no holiday camp here believe me,
no one smiles or sings, there are no games
beyond the extended waiting for your name
to be called. Kids sleep under lock and key,
dreaming a life where they are nobody.
Days are a joyless grind, always the same,
confined within the rules that we disclaim.
We holiday in camps abroad beside the sea,
equate our leisure with our right to be,
we swim in spotless pools and dine sans shame,
our wallets fat, refusing to feel blame,
defensive. We are willing detainees,
incarcerated, yet there is no fence
to hold us, we squander independence.

Night Bus

Travelling in hope, a child mother stares at her phone
willing it to ring; she lays her head on the pane,
surrenders to the squalor while her sallow baby sleeps,
indifferent to the sick and indigent clamouring at the doors
bathed in the orange sodium glare.

It is too late to be abroad in the city where we are all
equally blessed and cursed; barely able, biddable,
eyes shut tight against the light, ears deafened by
the raucous laughter learned in pubs.

City lights can't hide the shapes of bodies cowering
as we pass; bus shelters harbour the hospitals' surfeit,
doorways house the hostels' detritus,
beggars own the sweepings of the street.

Inchicore passed, the girl is losing patience as we stall
between St. Michael's and the South Circular Road.
On Camden Street, in traffic at a crawl, she grips
the handle of the pram but does not stand;
the doors hiss open, close, another wave of souls
tramp down the stairs.

I swallow bile and wish her phone would ring. I wish
the bus would turn around, but know we can't go back;
over the intercom the driver counsels and cajoles:
put out those cigarettes, we're almost there.
I think: We're almost home.

A Map

all he has is a map
    in his head
of a few crooked fields
    scarred by train tracks
    hemmed in by salt water
and a burgeoning town

sometimes he goes back there
    to pick at the past
to leave the imprint of
    his shoe in old mud
    the sea wind on his face
with his back to the town

he walks the few miles
    in his dreams
till he comes to the house
    back to front now
    since the road moved
concealing its sacred junk

he opens the back door
    never the front
and steps into the past
    affected by pity and love
    for those who lived there
with him once now all gone

the map is a child's drawing
    scrawled crayon
on raw nerves etched in guilt
    carefully rolled by an adult
    a scroll from a story where
x denotes buried treasure

In My Day

And always when I tell you how things were
you sigh and shake your head and I feel young;
inverse intimations of a future when I'll need you
more than you need me. For now, it is pretence:
I am the adult, you the child,
but still I ransack memory for signs of misery,
kid myself we always drank from jam jars,
not just that summer day when we sat
on the grass flicking gluttonous wasps
off jam sandwiches, swigging tea
from jars we'd used to catch pinkeens.

But when you say you do not need a lift,
that friends will bring you home,
I wonder has a rift appeared between us.
You read my furrowed brow and laugh at me,
remind me how I crossed the city alone
by bus when I was half your age.
I know you mean to tease, and I can see the joke,
the clever way you use my hard-boiled memoirs.
I've seen it all before, the need to break away
from those you love; dependence undervalued,
independence not yet earned.

Foundations shake, childhood certainties
collapse like high rise squats on news reports
from distant cities. I tell myself again that this is home.
I'm standing on the fault line of your life –
the ground is opening up but we are still the same;
everything else has changed. But that's another lie I tell myself.
In my day parents felt the same as I do now
and kids the same as you. This doesn't help.
I look from clock to door and suddenly feel old,
but not old enough to make free with the future
the way I have with the past.

Home

Once upon a time
I called it home,
a haven from my childish fears,
but soon it lost its shine,
became merely the place
where I practised
a studied disinterest.
Later, when they died,
it became property
harbouring objective value.

Once it was a magnet
with the power to hold
me between the fixed points
of two small towns; a bungalow
that seemed to tower,
a small house
crammed with kids,
alive with memories,
riddled with regret
for things not said.

This is how I aged:
I pushed the past away
as if it smelled of something bad;
I craved that distance from
my source when grown,
then wandered aimlessly
until I found
a semblance of the things
I never understood
but scorned.

Balancing Act

My father came from the north, from an avid race,
their history a guttural mumble of townlands and churches;
their new home a green field half-hidden by rocks
and gorse and bog water, shadowed by black hills,
backs turned on their old Caledonian homes.
Crude boats on grey water carried them here
to new inhospitable lands.

My mother came from the midlands,
by the shores of grand lakes where pleasure boats cruise;
one aunt a stern nun in the Far East
turned her back on her calling,
another ran guns for the rebels in the first Troubles;
a brother drowned in a capsule in the Baltic
when the war had already ended.

Their stories are real to my mind, as real as my own.
I relive them again to hold onto a past
that is slipping from me every day. I think myself modern,
I relish technology; my brother who lives in Lusaka beams
into my home, and we talk of the times we had pots
under beds to piss in, jam jars to drink from,
a hand pump for water at the end of the lane by our house.

My children are happy but urban and thin,
they speak with inquisitive irony
when describing the world as it is, real or virtual;
their futures are mapped out before them,
inverted histories set in geological stone:
the world is their village and they speak the language,
and I am the axis balancing future and past.

The Man, The Boy And The Map

The man decided he would draw a map
so that his son would never become lost.
He wanted so much for his little boy
and worried he would sometimes lack
the fortitude to keep hold of his hand.
He felt his days go past him like the wind.

All year their house was blasted by the wind,
an island place not shown on any map,
that's why the father drew his own by hand:
the record of their lives would not be lost.
The boy would sometimes think of things he lacked,
but judged himself a fairly happy boy

although he would have liked a friend, a boy,
another name to shout into the wind,
to help him take his mind off what he lacked.
He liked to think his life a kind of map
of secret ways and private paths long lost
to others, unguided by a hand

as warm and work-worn as his father's hand
who, after his wife's death, had raised the boy
alone; who struggled with his loss,
awake all night and listening to the wind,
poring over bill or book or map,
thinking of his son and what they lacked.

Sometimes they managed to forget their lack
when they walked the island hand in hand
over rugged hillsides with the map
the man had drawn to help him guide the boy.
The words they shared were scattered by the wind,
and meaning and intention were all lost.

And though the two were safe and never lost,
they could not speak the truth of what they lacked,
but felt it in the ever-cutting wind
and in the press of hand on tender hand.
The father sensed an absence in the boy,
the son clung tightly to the folded map.

The man and boy walked onward hand in hand,
not lost, but never naming what they lacked,
until a hungry wind devoured the map.

Gerry Asleep

Stretched out on the floor
in front of the fire
he sleeps in t-shirt and jeans
as I try to describe
his iambic breath
the result of crude labour
and vigorous thought

a truer poem than I could ever write

Lessons

(for Martha)

In the yard the children
form straight lines and wait
in expectation of the class;
the first constraint – the first sign
of the hand of man upon the face of God
after the fall in Eden.

I watch your peerless image fade,
eclipsed by Plato's puppet forms.
A door closes (perhaps another opens
somewhere in return), and you are gone.
The morning's mine to think of you
and wait till half past one.

I hear the angels' voices rise and fall,
benediction through an open window.
And then a sudden tumult, an energy released,
the angels beat their wings upon the glass
until the gates of heaven open and you are there
before me, smiling, telling me your life.

Your little hand in mine,
we walk the quarter mile in silence,
just two amid a stream of others,
part of the crowd, but separate.
You run ahead when we draw near our street,
the fallen leaves are gold stars at your feet.

The Kitchen In Winter

From muggy beds we dragged our sullen selves
and braved the freezing air
in rooms where windows rattled
when the goods trains passed.
Smoke and steam coughed up in clouds
from the ancient range
and on the hob a pot or two, a kettle singing.
The house an aged and ailing corpus;
extremities exposed and frozen,
we gravitated towards the beating heart
like blood and oxygen, without choice,
because that's how it was.

A table, chairs, brown bread
and tea as dark as oil,
and over all the wireless, those pips,
the fleeting fear of silence,
the endless weather we had then.
And us, from nowhere all at once surrounding her,
demanding, standing, sitting, eating, drinking,
talking until the clock's hands drew attention
to the lateness of the hour
and we were gone.
The radio spoke while the clock
ticked our absence away.

Orienteering

Even if you found
your way back home
what difference would it make?
There's no one there;
the people and
the place that held you close –
embraced or restrained
(you never were sure which) –
the words they said,
have all dissolved
in time.
All that remains
is a Sunday coat and
matching scarf,
a battered hat
and a penknife that
peeled apples
in one go,
cleaned fingernails
and tamped tobacco
down in a pipe bowl.
If you sketched
a map from memory
you'd maybe see
the broad outline
of staggering events,
or feel the smart
of tiny hurts
absurdly magnified
as you move away.
The world gets smaller
as you grow,
the days turn faster
as you age,
it makes you think
the present is recoiling
from the past
and the history
you carry
in your heart.

When We Were Small

The thing we loved the most when we were small
was opening our presents in the dark;
the days were short, the tree was very tall

and from bright paper fell a new football
or cars that raced on magic that made sparks.
The thing we loved the most when we were small

was waking up our parents with our calls
of "Santy's come! Wake up!" The dog would bark,
the days were short, the tree was very tall

when we believed that God cared for us all
and angels urged us shepherds still to hark
to the things we loved the most when we were small.

This is the way we live after the fall,
grown up in knowledge but by faith unmarked.
The days were short, the tree was very tall

when we accepted God was all in all
and Christmas was the time we chose to mark
the things we loved the most when we were small,
when days were short and the tree was very tall.

The Days

We pass the days in offices where windows
are locked shut and air is blown through dusty vents
into a pool of light where no one speaks.
The drone of blocked machines lives in our heads –
the rush of ocean over sea stones, shells
crunching under carpeted feet – we
move between workstation, photocopier
and toilet. Close eyes, breathe and press delete.
Even the weeping ash can meet the wind
and let her hair blow back from off her face.
Our blind hands brush a sheaf of dead reports,
bathed in a pool of sallow light, and when we breathe
it is the same air every time, same dust,
same flakes of skin: we pass the days like this.

Photograph: Martha Kirk

BRIAN KIRK is an award winning poet and short story writer from Clondalkin in Dublin. He was selected for the Poetry Ireland Introductions Series in 2013 and was shortlisted for the Patrick Kavanagh Award in 2014 and 2015. He won the Jonathan Swift Creative Writing Award for Poetry in 2014, the Bailieborough Poetry Prize in 2015 and the Galway RCC Poetry Award in 2016. His poetry film *Red Line Haiku* was featured at the Red Line Book Festival in October 2015 and was subsequently shortlisted for the Ó Bhéal Poetry Film Competition in 2016. His poetry has been widely published and has been nominated for the Forward Prize and Pushcart Prize. His novel for 9-12 year olds *The Rising Son* was published in December 2015. He is a member of the Hibernian Poetry Workshop and he blogs at www.briankirkwriter.com.